BLUE BANNER BIOGRAPHY

Blake
SHELTON

Mitchell Lane
PUBLISHERS

P.O. Box 196
Hockessin, Delaware 19707
Visit us on the web: www.mitchelllane.com
Comments? Email us: mitchelllane@mitchelllane.com

Risa Brown

Printing   1   2   3   4   5   6   7   8   9

Blue Banner Biographies

Abby Wambach	Ice Cube	Miguel Tejada
Adele	Ja Rule	Mike Trout
Alicia Keys	Jamie Foxx	Nancy Pelosi
Allen Iverson	Jason Derulo	Natasha Bedingfield
Ashanti	Jay-Z	Nicki Minaj
Ashlee Simpson	Jennifer Hudson	One Direction
Ashton Kutcher	Jennifer Lopez	Orianthi
Avril Lavigne	Jessica Simpson	Orlando Bloom
Blake Lively	J. K. Rowling	P. Diddy
Blake Shelton	Joe Flacco	Peyton Manning
Bow Wow	John Legend	Pink
Brett Favre	Justin Berfield	Pit Bull
Britney Spears	Justin Timberlake	Prince William
Bruno Mars	Kanye West	Queen Latifah
CC Sabathia	Kate Hudson	Rihanna
Carrie Underwood	Katy Perry	Robert Downey Jr.
Chris Brown	Keith Urban	Robert Pattinson
Chris Daughtry	Kelly Clarkson	Ron Howard
Christina Aguilera	Kenny Chesney	Sean Kingston
Ciara	Ke$ha	Selena
Clay Aiken	Kevin Durant	Shakira
Cole Hamels	Kristen Stewart	Shia LaBeouf
Condoleezza Rice	Lady Gaga	Shontelle Layne
Corbin Bleu	Lance Armstrong	Soulja Boy Tell 'Em
Daniel Radcliffe	Leona Lewis	Stephenie Meyer
David Ortiz	Lil Wayne	Taylor Swift
David Wright	Lionel Messi	T.I.
Derek Jeter	Lindsay Lohan	Timbaland
Drew Brees	LL Cool J	Tim McGraw
Eminem	Ludacris	Tim Tebow
Eve	Mariah Carey	Toby Keith
Fergie	Mario	Usher
Flo Rida	Mary J. Blige	Vanessa Anne Hudgens
Gwen Stefani	Mary-Kate and Ashley Olsen	Will.i.am
Hope Solo	Megan Fox	Zac Efron

Library of Congress Cataloging-in-Publication Data
Brown, Risa W.
 Blake Shelton / by Risa Brown.
     pages cm
Includes bibliographical references and index.
 ISBN 978-1-61228-641-9 (library bound)
1. Shelton, Blake—Juvenile literature. 2. Country musicians—Biography—Juvenile literature. I. Title.
ML3930.S485B53 2014
782.421642092—dc23
[B]
                                                                          2014020457

eBook ISBN: 9781612286655

ABOUT THE AUTHOR: Risa Brown is the author of twelve books for children and three for librarians. She has been a children's or school librarian for twenty-three years. She now writes full-time and lives in Arlington, Texas. She sings in a community chorus and loves to travel.

Blake Shelton, country music star and judge on the hit show The Voice, appears regularly at the American Country Music Awards.

Healing in the Heartland

On May 20, 2013, a powerful tornado hit Moore, Oklahoma. Thousands of homes were completely destroyed. Thousands more were damaged. Some of those buildings were elementary schools and the town hospital. People were killed, even children.

The whole country watched in horror and wanted to help. Blake Shelton, country music star and judge on the hit NBC show *The Voice*, quickly sprang into action.

Just two days after the tornado Blake and his wife Miranda Lambert performed the hit song "Over You" on *The Voice*. This song was special to Blake and Miranda. They had written it to honor Blake's older brother, Richie, who was killed in a 1990 car crash when Blake was just fourteen. Their performance helped get donations for the Red Cross, an organization that is always on the scene of disasters to help people.

That wasn't enough for Blake. Less than two weeks after the disaster, he organized a benefit concert to raise more money for the tornado victims. So many other artists were willing to participate that the concert was sure to be a hit. He named it "Healing in the Heartland."

"Everyone has their way to help and mine as an entertainer is to perform to help raise money and awareness for this tragedy," Blake said in a press release before the benefit.

To Blake, these victims were neighbors. He was born and raised in Ada, Oklahoma. He and Miranda lived in Tishomingo, only a hundred miles from Moore. They couldn't sit by and do nothing.

> *"Everyone has their way to help and mine as an entertainer is to perform to help raise money and awareness for this tragedy," Blake said in a press release before the benefit.*

One of his "Healing in the Heartland" guests was Reba McIntyre. She and Blake had previously teamed up in 2011 to help victims of a tornado that ravaged Atoka County, Oklahoma. But 2013's "Healing in the Heartland" was a much bigger event. For one, the need was greater because the tornado had done so much damage. For another, Blake was a bigger star. Because of his growing success and his work on *The Voice*, he had many new fans that rallied around his cause.

Blake opened the program with "God Gave Me You."

Before singing "Threaten Me with Heaven" Vince Gill said, "I'd like to do this song for twenty-four people that didn't make it," referring to those who had died in the tornado.

Miranda almost cried when pictures of lost pets were flashed on the screen while she sang "The House That Built Me."

Blake and R&B artist Usher perform the duet "Home" as scenes of the devastation in Moore, Oklahoma, are shown during "Healing in the Heartland."

Blake and R&B artist Usher closed the concert by singing a duet of "Home."

The event not only raised money with ticket sales but during the benefit's broadcast on NBC viewers could call in and donate money. Within hours, "Healing in the Heartland" had raised $6 million. "Home" was later released as a download that continues to raise funds for Moore and its residents.

All the money raised went to the United Way of Central Oklahoma May Tornadoes Relief Fund. This special agency promised to help victims immediately and continue helping for however long it took to rebuild their community.

Blake and his mother, Dorothy Shackleford. Dorothy also writes songs, some with her famous son.

Small Town Dreams

For Blake, "Healing in the Heartland" was all about home. Oklahoma will always be home. And no matter where Blake travels or how far, home and family are very important to him.

Blake Tollison Shelton was born in Ada, Oklahoma, on June 18, 1976. His mother Dorothy ran a beauty salon. His father Dick sold used cars. Blake was the youngest of three children. In addition to his brother Richie, he also had an older sister Endy.

Ada is a small town in southern Oklahoma. There was not a lot to do there. Blake loved being outside.

"From the day he could walk," Dorothy said on the Great American Country (GAC) channel series *Backstory*, "[Blake] would get up every morning, jump into a pair of shorts—no shirt, no shoes—run outside, and start climbing trees."

He was especially fascinated with animals and frequently brought home whatever he could catch. He found an aquarium in a dumpster for the crawdads, tadpoles, frogs, lizards, and snakes that he caught. He told

CMTNews.com that he even had a pet turkey named Turkey.

Blake especially looked up to his brother, Richie, who was ten years older. Richie had a record collection and loved country music. "Everything he did was the coolest thing in the world and I wanted to be him," Blake admitted to GAC. "He was a superhero to me."

Blake pretended to be a country star and sang at the top of his lungs. Dorothy decided to channel her son's creative energy into performances.

Blake pretended to be a country star and sang at the top of his lungs. Dorothy decided to channel her son's creative energy into performances. The only talent show she could find was a beauty pageant, which really embarrassed him. Later when he learned to play the guitar, Dorothy recorded a tape and sent it to a local theatre called Music Palace. They loved Blake's singing and scheduled him to perform. Blake surprised everyone with his lively rendition of "Old Time Rock and Roll." From then on, Blake knew he wanted to be a country star.

He began to perform regularly all over Ada. Music also helped him cope with Dorothy and Dick ending their marriage. Blake told GAC that his parents' divorce was one of the hardest things he had to get through. But, Blake added, his father always made time to spend with Blake and his siblings.

Part of Blake's signature stage look early in his career was his mullet hairstyle, which was short on top and the sides but long in the back. He wore his hair the same way for many years even though some people made fun of it.

One day in 1990 everything changed. Blake's father came to his high school, got Blake out of class, and told him Richie had been killed in an accident. "It was the second time I saw my dad crying," Blake said on *Backstory*, adding that the news was like "a gunshot to the head."

Dick told GAC he could see how serious Blake became after the accident. "You don't get over that. Nobody does. You learn to live with it."

"I started realizing how lucky every day is you get and I was determined to make this life count," Blake added.

Blake's parents gave him Richie's album collection. "I just listened to them over and over again to feel like he was there," Blake told *The Associated Press*. As he listened, Blake became more focused than ever to become a country star. He sang and played when other kids were going to the movies. Then in 1992 he won the Denbo Diamond award, which honors Oklahoma's top young performer. The recognition made him a local celebrity when he was just sixteen.

A short time later he happened to be the entertainment at a ceremony honoring Mae Boren Axton, a very famous Nashville songwriter who was also born in Ada. Blake recalled to GAC that after she heard him sing, Mae told him: "You've got a long way to go but I think you should consider moving to Nashville and giving this a shot. I'll help you any way I can."

So two weeks after Blake graduated from Ada High School he moved to Nashville assuming success was going to be easy. He told GAC he remembers thinking, "People in Ada like me. Surely I can take over Nashville in no time."

He soon found out making a name for himself wasn't easy at all.

Blake got a lot of criticism about his hairstyle, called a mullet. For years, he stubbornly stuck to his long hair and cowboy hat.

Ups and Downs

*B*lake admits he was naive when he moved to Nashville—both professionally and personally. He had no experience taking care of himself. "I thought I'd be a big star and however they made money is how I was going to make money. I'd never even paid a bill before," he said in a GAC interview.

He called Mae Boren Axton. Not only did she introduce him to people in country music, she hired him to paint her house.

For three years, Blake did odd jobs and wrote songs for different music companies. He talked to a lot of people and gave away a lot of demos, but he couldn't find anyone to give him a break. Blake told GAC how discouraged he was, at times thinking, "Maybe this isn't what I'm supposed to do. Maybe I need to grow up and get real."

But he stubbornly held on and kept trying.

Then he met the right person. Bobby Braddock, a well-known songwriter in Nashville, liked Blake so much that he got him a recording contract with Giant Records in 1998. Even with a contract, it was four long years before they released his first single. When "Austin" finally came out, it topped the country music chart and stayed at number one for five weeks.

Then Giant Records went out of business. Warner Brothers bought some of Giant's contracts and Blake's was one of them. His new label helped him release his first album called simply *Blake Shelton*.

> **Blake was at a crossroads. He wanted to succeed but what worked for him in the past was not working now. He decided to reinvent himself musically.**

Everyone had high hopes for Blake's next two singles, "All Over You" and "Ol' Red," but neither one sold well. Because of that Warner Brothers did not want to make a video of either song. Blake recalled to GAC how he risked everything, telling the label, "If you'll do a video for 'Ol' Red' and that song does not become a hit, I'll walk away. Y'all can drop me from Warner Brothers Records and you'll never hear from me again."

The gamble worked. The video and single helped his debut album earn gold status, which is when an album sells 500,000 copies or more. His career looked bright and he made plans for the future. He proposed to his high school sweetheart, Kaynette Williams, who he married in 2003. That same year he recorded another album called "The Dreamer."

Sales of the singles on his second album went down. He got criticized about everything. His hair was too long. He always wore a hat. His sarcastic sense of humor sometimes rubbed people the wrong way.

Blake was at a crossroads. He wanted to succeed but what worked for him in the past was not working now. He decided to reinvent himself musically. He began to look for songs that reflected his personality and feelings, not just what others thought would be a hit. He wanted to be himself so he could perform honestly.

He also examined what made a good performance. At that time, he was opening for Rascal Flatts. He watched them and analyzed what they did to put on an exciting show. He instructed his band not to simply stand motionless in front of the microphone and Blake started moving more around stage. He looked at every aspect of himself and followed his instincts. He even decided it was time to cut his hair.

Unfortunately, his marriage to Kaynette ended in 2006. He calls that time "the darkest point" of his life. The songs he wanted to sing were dark and depressing. His album, *Pure BS*, was criticized for being too sad. He sold the farm outside of Nashville where he and Kaynette lived and moved back to Oklahoma.

"I didn't realize how empty I was on the inside until I got back home," he recollected to GAC.

As part of his love for his home state, Blake organized an event he called *Raindance* and held it in Ada. It was a combination archery tournament, team roping competition, and concert. The second year he raised $100,000 to benefit families hurt by wildfires and tornadoes. He didn't take credit for the money that was raised. He told GAC, "I am truly amazed at the generosity of my fellow Oklahomans, helping a neighbor in need by attending and participating in Raindance."

After Blake became more famous, CMT News asked him in an interview, "What is some advice for a young guy who wants to do what you are doing?"

Blake answered: "The only real good advice I have is to move to Nashville and be prepared to be told 'no' so many times that it makes you sick because that's what is going to happen when you get there. People are gonna tell you you're not good enough, or they're not even gonna talk to you, period. It takes time and it takes patience."

He also talked about how much people had helped him. The struggle had been hard on him in many ways but he had learned a lot.

Things slowly turned around with his career and his personal life. Blake began to date Miranda Lambert. She was a fellow country music artist and they had a lot in common.

Miranda also influenced his music. She convinced Blake to record "Home," a song written by Michael Bublé. It became Blake's fourth number one single.

"We love to fish and hunt, drive around back roads, listen to music, and sit on the tailgate with a cooler. Literally what people think about the songs is what we do," Miranda told GAC.

"It should be illegal how much fun we have when we're home," Blake added. "She is a person who can relate to me in a way very few people in the world can."

Miranda also influenced his music. She convinced Blake to record "Home," a song written by Michael Bublé. It became Blake's fourth number one single. Miranda also suggested that Trace Adkins should do a duet with Blake on "Hillbilly Bone." It became another number one single, earning awards for both Blake and Trace.

Blake and Trace Adkins (right) have been friends for years.

His next single, "She Wouldn't Be Gone," from his fifth album *Startin' Fires*, also became a number one hit. Blake felt he could finally relax.

In 2010 Blake Shelton earned the biggest honor in country music when he was inducted into the Grand Ole Opry. His good friend Trace Adkins introduced him at the ceremony. A month later, Blake was named Male Vocalist of the Year at the Country Music Awards. Blake was on a roll.

After all this excitement, Blake spent time at his home in Tishomingo to clear his head. "I just started thinking about my life and all the dumb things I've done and how I could be better. As I was cleaning out my garage, I felt like I was doing that with my life," Blake told GAC. "It just hit me. I've got to ask Miranda to marry me."

Blake and wife Miranda at the 53rd Annual Grammy Awards in Los Angeles, California.

CHAPTER 4

On an Incredible Roll

"I thought I'd never be one of those people that just got on a roll like I'm on right now. I don't know how it happened. But I hope it stays that way," Blake Shelton told GAC.

Blake has been the first one to say he is incredibly lucky. He also has a knack for surrounding himself with people who can help him and turning them into good friends. He downplays how hard he had to work to get where he is.

He and Miranda married on May 14, 2011. He says his marriage to Miranda gives him stability and grounding. The depth of his connection to Miranda became even more public when they wrote the song "Over You."

They were watching television one night and happened to see an episode of GAC's program *Backstory* about Blake. Seeing his dad talk about his brother's death made Blake and Miranda talk about how important Richie had been and how his death hit Blake hard. That night, Blake shared his feelings about Richie's death, and the best way they could deal with it was to write a song.

Because the song was so personal, Blake didn't think he could sing it on stage. He asked Miranda if she would sing it. She recorded it and the song was so popular it won Song of the Year at the Academy of Country Music Awards held in April 2013.

Another reason "Over You" was so hard for Blake was that his father had died on January 17, 2012, not long after they finished writing the song. Dick suffered from emphysema, a lung disease that makes breathing difficult and steadily weakens the body. In Dick's final months, Blake flew home whenever he could to be with his father and tried to stay strong for him. Blake always gives his dad credit for inspiring "Over You."

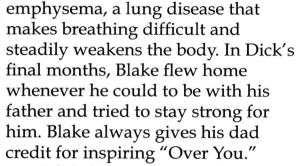

While his country music success kept growing, another opportunity knocked on Blake's door: to be a judge and coach for The Voice.

While his country music success kept growing, another opportunity knocked on Blake's door: to be a judge and coach for *The Voice*. The TV series became a hit show that introduced him to an audience outside of country music. His personality and crazy sense of humor won him many new fans. The Grand Ole Opry website called Blake "one of the best ambassadors the country music genre has ever had" because of his popularity on the NBC talent show.

Mark Burnett, one of the executive producers of *The Voice*, wanted a country music category when he developed the series. He told GAC he always felt that Blake was the "totally obvious cool choice." But Blake was not interested. He rejected their offers until he heard that Christina Aguilera would be on the show. Her presence won him over. The other judges on *The Voice* in its first season were

The original team of judges for The Voice. From left:
Carson Daly, CeeLo Green, Adam Levine, Christina
Aguilera, and Blake.

rapper CeeLo Green and Adam Levine, lead vocalist for the band Maroon 5.

Once again, Blake's outgoing personality quickly won the other artists over. Despite their different backgrounds they became friends. Blake's friendship, especially with Adam, has added an extra element of good-natured rivalry to the show.

According to the NBC website, *The Voice* is a unique talent competition with four different phases. There are the blind auditions, which allow the judges to choose someone based on their voice and not on their looks. The judges then coach their chosen singers to prepare for the battle rounds, guiding them through the eliminations. In the knock-out

On the stage of The Voice. *From left: Blake, Carson Daly, Christina Aguilera, executive producer Mark Burnett, CeeLo Green, and Adam Levine.*

Different seasons of The Voice *had different coaches. During seasons four and six, the coaches were (from left) Adam Levine, Shakira, Usher and Blake.*

rounds, each singer must impress his or her own coach. The candidates who survive that round make it to the finals. The winner is chosen by the TV audience who vote during a live broadcast.

Blake is generous but tough as a coach, funny and down-home as a judge. Fellow judge Usher said to TasteofCountry.com, "He's a great coach, and he's really taught me a lot. [He is] also kind of giving lessons to America about what it takes to be an artist."

Even after his contestants win Blake continues to help them, proving again that he's as generous as he is talented.

Blake keeps winning awards! In 2013, he won Male Vocalist of the Year for the second time.

Happy and Thankful

Blake Shelton seems to be everywhere right now—touring, winning awards, hosting benefits, and being on television. Yet even with all these things in his life, Blake is first and foremost a performer.

"I'm a country singer," Blake told GAC. "I'm a country artist. At the end of the day that's who I am and that's what I want to do with my life." Blake has built his life around country music and he won't let television or anything else distract him from it. He will also let that guide him in the future.

That was his philosophy when he made his album, *Based on a True Story*.... Blake said on GrandOleOpry.com that he had been happy with his previous album, *Red River Blue*. But as he thought about a follow-up he went song by song, picking tunes that he liked, getting fellow artists to participate, and performing them the best he could. "The next thing you know we had built something terrific."

Blake has frequent "meet and greets" with his fans. Here he signs a fan's guitar.

Chuck Dauphin from *Billboard* called *Based on a True Story...* "all about getting personal," and Joseph Hudak from *Country Weekly* said the ballads are "where Blake excels and the avowed smart aleck is found with his heart on his denim sleeve."

But Blake is more than a country singer. When he won Male Vocalist of the Year, not only did he feel pride in how far he'd come, he felt like he had a new responsibility. "If I'm male vocalist of the year," Blake explained to GAC, "then it must mean that I'm one of those people now that gets to decide if [country music] moves forward and if it moves on."

Blake has been called an ambassador of country music because he has introduced the genre and its artists to a wider audience. Not only does he nurture new talent, he encourages performers and writers to work together. He and Miranda have a recording studio in their home and frequently invite artists to use their studio and have jam sessions.

Blake also takes seriously his ability to help people, as "Healing in the Heartland" proved. In December 2013, he teamed up with J.C. Penney to raise funds for the United Service Organization, or USO, which helps American troops and their families. Blake appeared in a commercial for the USO where video images of spouses and children of service men and women joined him in singing "Silent Night."

After all the struggles he endured to break into country music, Blake is appreciative for all his blessings and loves his life.

He said on GrandOleOpry.com, "I'm happy and thankful and I want to sound like that in my record."

He says he has learned some valuable lessons. Be true to yourself. Love family and friends wholeheartedly. Help young performers. Be generous with people in need.

And represent country music everywhere he goes.

1976   Born June 18 in Ada, Oklahoma

1984   Performs "Old Time Rock and Roll" at a local talent show

1985   Parents divorce

1990   Older brother Richie Shelton dies in car accident July 31

1992   Wins the Denbo Diamond award at age 16

1994   Moves to Nashville; Mae Boren Axton helps him get a job as a songwriter; gets first recording contract

2001   Signs with Giant Records; his first solo single, "Austin," is number one for five weeks; he is invited to play at the Grand Ole Opry

2003   Releases second album, *The Dreamer,* in February with the number one single "The Baby"

2006   Begins dating Miranda Lambert

2007   Releases fourth album, *Pure BS*; Blake appears as a judge on *Nashville Star* and *Clash of the Choirs*

2008   Releases his fourth No. 1 single, "Home."

2009   Releases fifth album, *Startin' Fires,* including a duet with Miranda; releases a duet with Trace Adkins titled "Hillbilly Bone."

2010   Releases "Hillbilly Bone" and an album of greatest hits; joins the Grand Ole Opry; wins Male Vocalist of the Year at the Country Music Awards

2011   Joins *The Voice* as a judge and coach; marries Miranda Lambert on May 14; "Honey Bee" single earns gold status quicker than any other recording by a male country star

2012   Blake's father Dick dies on January 17; performs "America the Beautiful" with Miranda at the Super Bowl

2013   Releases his eighth album; "Mine Would Be You" becomes Blake's tenth consecutive number one single; organizes the "Healing in the Heartland" Relief Benefit Concert on May 29

2014   "Doin' What She Likes" becomes Blake's eleventh consecutive number one hit and sets a record for the most consecutive number one hits

DISCOGRAPHY

Albums

2001	*Blake Shelton*
2003	*The Dreamer*
2004	*Blake Shelton's Barn and Grill*
2007	*Pure BS*
2008	*Startin' Fires*
2011	*Red River Blue*
2012	*Cheers, It's Christmas*
2013	*Based on a True Story...*

#1 Singles

2001	"Austin"
2002	"The Baby"
2004	"Some Beach"

#1 Singles (*continued*)

2008	"Home"
	"She Wouldn't Be Gone"
2009	"I'll Just Hold On"
	"Hillbilly Bone"
	"All About Tonight"
2010	"Who Are You When I'm Not Looking"
2011	"Honey Bee"
	"God Gave Me You"
2012	"Drink on It"
	"Over You"
2013	"Sure Be Cool If You Did"

AWARDS

2010

Academy of Country Music Vocal Event of the Year, "Hillbilly Bone" (with Trace Adkins)

CMT Music Awards Collaborative Video of the Year, "Hillbilly Bone" (with Trace Adkins)

Country Music Association Vocal Event of the Year, "Hillbilly Bone" (with Trace Adkins)

2011

CMT Music Awards Male Video of the Year, "Who Are You When I'm Not Looking"

CMT Music Awards Best Web Video of the Year, "Kiss My Country @#!%"

Country Music Association Male Vocalist of the Year

American Music Awards Favorite Country Male Artist

2012

CMT Teddy Awards Best Flirting Video, "Honey Bee"

Academy of Country Music Awards Male Vocalist of the Year

2012 (*continued*)

Country Music Association Entertainer of the Year

Country Music Association Male Vocalist of the Year

Country Music Association Song of the Year

2013

Academy of Country Music Awards Song of the Year, "Over You"

Gene Weed Special Achievement Award

CMT Music Awards Male Vocalist of the Year, "Sure Be Cool if You Did"

Country Music Association Awards Male Vocalist of the Year

Country Music Association Awards Album of the Year, *Based on a True Story...*

American Country Awards Album of the Year, *Based on a True Story...*

American Country Awards Single by a Male Artist, "Sure Be Cool if You Did"

American Country Awards Great American Country, Music Video of the Year, "Sure Be Cool if You Did"

American Country Awards Music Video by a Male Artist, "Sure Be Cool if You Did"

FURTHER READING

Books

Tieck, Sarah. *Adam Levine.* Minneapolis, MN: Abdo Publishing Co., 2014.

Tieck, Sarah. *Blake Shelton.* Minneapolis, MN: Abdo Publishing Co., 2013.

Wheelwright, Wayne. *The Blake Shelton Quiz Book.* Luton, UK: Andrews UK (Kindle), 2013.

On the Internet

Official Blake Shelton website
    http://www.blakeshelton.com
Grand Ole Opry
    http://www.opry.com
Billboard
    http://www.billboard.com
Taste of Country
    http://tasteofcountry.com

Works Consulted

"20 Questions with Blake Shelton." *CMT.* February 14. 2014. http://www.cmt.com/news/20-questions/1459805/20-questions-with-blake-shelton.jhtml

"Blake Organizing 'Healing in the Heartland: Relief Benefit Concert." Blake Shelton Official website. February 14, 2014. http://www.blakeshelton.com/news/blake-organizing-healing-heartland-relief-benefit-concert-279856

"Blake Shelton," *Grand Ole Opry.* February 14, 2014. http://www.opry.com/artist/blake-shelton

"Blake Shelton's Backstory." *YouTube.* February 14, 2014. http://www.youtube.com/watch?v=0Z223KSs3tA

"Blake Shelton's Raindance is a Huge Success." Great American Country. May 7, 2007. http://www.gactv.com/gac/nw_headlines/article/0,,gac_26063_5524721,00.html

Dauphin, Chuck. "Blake Shelton, 'Based on a True Story…'Track by Track Review," *Billboard*. February 14, 2014. http://www.billboard.com/articles/review/1554485/blake-shelton-based-on-a-true-story-track-by-track-review

Hudak, Joseph. *"Based on a True Story…by Blake Shelton."* *Country Weekly*. February 14, 2014. http://www.countryweekly.com/reviews/based-true-story-blake-shelton

Leahey, Andrew. "Blake Shelton biography." *Billboard*. February 14, 2014. http://www.billboard.com/artist/289793/blake-shelton/biography

Mannette, Alice. "Oklahoma Tornado 2013 Devastates Moore, Kills Dozens." *Huffington Post*. February 14, 2014. http://www.huffingtonpost.com/2013/05/20/oklahoma-tornado-2013_n_3309844.html

"Over You by Miranda Lambert." *Songfacts*. February 14, 2014. http://www.songfacts.com/detail.php?id=24508

Paxman, Bob. "Blake Shelton's 'Healing in the Heartland' Raises $6 Million for Tornado Victims."*Country Weekly*. May 31, 2013. http://www.countryweekly.com/news/blake-sheltons-healing-heartland-raises-6-million-tornado-victims

Rogers, Christopher. "Blake Shelton and Usher Perform Duet at Tornado Benefit Concert." *Hollywood Life*. May 30, 2013. http://hollywoodlife.com/2013/05/30/healing-in-the-heartland-concert-blake-shelton- tornado/

"The Voice: About the Show." NBC. February 14, 2014. http://www.nbc.com/the-voice/about

Vinson, Christina. "Usher on Blake Shelton: He's a Great 'The Voice' Coach, but 'Somebody's Got to Tear Him Down.' " *Taste of Country*. February 14, 2014. http://tasteofcountry.com/usher-on-blake-shelton-tear-him-down

INDEX